Usborne
Sticker Dolly Dressing
Dogs & Puppies

Designed and illustrated by

Antonia Miller and Stella Baggott

Written by Fiona Watt

Contents

A new puppy

Megan and Ellie are choosing their new puppy. They're watching the litter of puppies to see how they play with each other. They are looking for a puppy that's friendly, playful and curious.

Megan

Ellie

Puppy party

It's Lauren's birthday and she's celebrating by meeting Elena and Alyssa in the park. Now that their puppies have been vaccinated, the dolls can walk them in the park and they can play with each other and meet other dogs.

Elena

Fern

Lauren

Alyssa

Roxy

Buddy

5

Dog boutique

Natalie and Lily are browsing the accessories, clothes and pampering products in a new boutique that has opened in town. Natalie's hoping to find a dog bowl for her puppy, Otto.

Lily

Otto

Natalie

7

Dog café

All dogs, puppies and their owners are welcome at the dog-friendly café, where they can relax and eat tasty treats. Even though Tilly doesn't have a dog of her own, she often goes to the café to meet dog-loving owners and their pets.

Tilly

Ruby

Alice

A walk in the woods

Olivia and Rosie are out walking Rosie's dog, Baxter. They've bumped into Izzy and her rescue dog, Lucky. The dogs are delighted to see each other and wag their tails wildly.

Olivia

Rosie

Baxter

Izzy

11

Training class

Sit... and stay! Mia, Lexie and Keira are learning how to train their dogs. Piper, Max and Coco already know to come when their names are called and now they are learning how to sit when they're told to.

Lexie

Mia

Piper

Max

Coco

Keira

Snowy walk

It snowed heavily last night, so Katya and Sophie are wrapped up in warm winter clothes. They've also put coats on their dogs to protect them from the icy wind.

Katya

Lola

Sophie

Daisy

Visiting the vet

Tanya has an appointment with the vet to have her puppy, Mitzy, microchipped. If Mitzy ever gets lost she can be scanned and Tanya's details will show up on the scanner.

Tanya

Jess

Alex

Ava

Polly

Playing in the park

Every morning the dolls meet with their dogs in the park. Molly, Kate's dog, loves to chase tennis balls, but Bracken is happy to stay close to Jade.

Molly

Asha

Jade

Kate

Bracken

Grooming salon

Ozzy's coat has been clipped and Jodie has washed him with a special dog shampoo that she's now rinsing away. Emma is trimming Belle's fur, but is styling it by leaving some parts longer than the rest.

Jodie

Ozzy

Emma

Belle

Dog show

This is the first year that Arianna, Holly and
Freya have entered the annual dog show.
The judges have awarded Cody 'Best in show'.

Arianna

Cody

Freya

Monty

Bonnie

Holly

Time for bed

Every night, Pepper the puppy curls up on the rug beside Millie's bed and falls asleep. He occasionally twitches and his paws quiver as he dreams of chasing squirrels.

A new puppy
Pages 2-3

Megan's outfit

Ellie's outfit

Puppy party
Pages 4-5

Elena's leggings and top

Lauren's top

Elena's dress

Elena's shoes

Alyssa's outfit

Training class
Pages 12-13

Keira's shoes

Keira's sweater

Lexie's top

Mia's cutoffs

Mia's sweater

Lola and Daisy's coats

Snowy walk
Pages 14-15

Sophie's hat

Katya's jacket and boots

Sophie's outfit

Visiting the vet
Pages 16-17

Tanya's outfit

Alex's top and pink shoes

Polly's outfit

Mitzy

Jess's top and boots

Dog show
Pages 22-23

Arianna's outfit

Holly's clothes

Freya's shirt

Time for bed
Page 24

Pepper